365 DAYS OF DOODLING

discovering the joys of
being creative every day

Carin Channing

INTENTIONAL PUBLISHING

copyright © 2015 by Carin Channing
(Text and illustrations)

Published by
Intentional Publishing
P.O. Box 55872
Seattle, WA 98155
www.intentionalpublishing.com
www.365daysofdoodling.com

Designer: Julie-Anne Graham
Back cover photo: Roger Casama II

All rights reserved. This book may not be reproduced in whole or in part without written permission from the publisher, except by a reviewer who may quote brief passages in a review; nor may any of this book be reproduced, stored in a retrieval system, or transmitted in any form or by any means, electronic, mechanical, photocopying, recording, or other, without written permission from the publisher.

Library of Congress Cataloguing-in-Publication Data on file with publisher

ISBN 978-0-9795356-0-4
First printing

for you

doo-dle

n. a simple, spontaneous creative expression

v. to create simply and spontaneously

Contents

- 1   My Story
- 7   How to Use this Book
- 8   Tools
- 10   Some Doodling Guidelines
- 17   The Prompts
- 384   Gratitude
- 386   Doodle Outreach

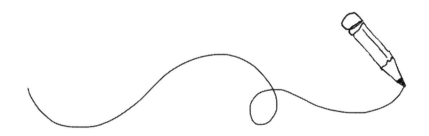

MY STORY

When I was a little girl, I loved coloring in coloring books. Coloring inside the lines soothed me. Besides, I thought I couldn't draw. I must have tried once or twice or a bunch, but what

I made didn't look "realistic," and I gave up on it.

I've always been a writer (I have a mug that says so), and I even play a little music and sing, but all things drawing eluded me...

until I was invited to a
30 day Doodle Challenge.

The invitation →

And within two weeks,
I lost track of the days.

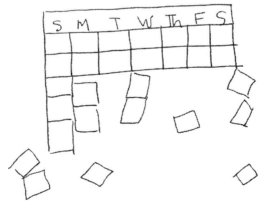

While making a doodle every day, I discovered

DOODLING IS:

easy
simple
fun
wise
fun
liberating
the best!
relaxing
revealing

fun
grounding
energizing
youthfulizing
clarifying
amazing
fun, fun, fun.

I loved it so much I started hosting doodle gatherings with people all over the world, and a good time was had by all.

Then I started doodling with strangers, and they loved it too!

I didn't want to limit doodle-tunities to those in my classes or who happen to meet me in line at the juice shop...

So here is my gift to you!

365 DAYS OF DOODLING

How to Use This Book

Use this book in whatever way is most FUN for you!

doodling alone is fun

doodling with friends is fun

You can follow the numbers in order...

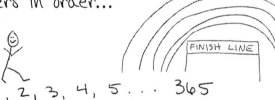

1, 2, 3, 4, 5 ... 365

Or make it a

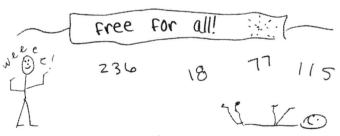

free for all!

236   18   77   115

TOOLS

To doodle directly in this book, try...

pencil

pastels

the beloved box of crayons

← Post-it notes on the pages

Or find a notebook you love and try...

paints

colored markers

writing pens

Some DOODLING guidelines

1. **make messes**

2. If you find yourself hesitating, keep diving in.

3. Be yourself.

If you find yourself comparing or criticizing, put it in the doodle!

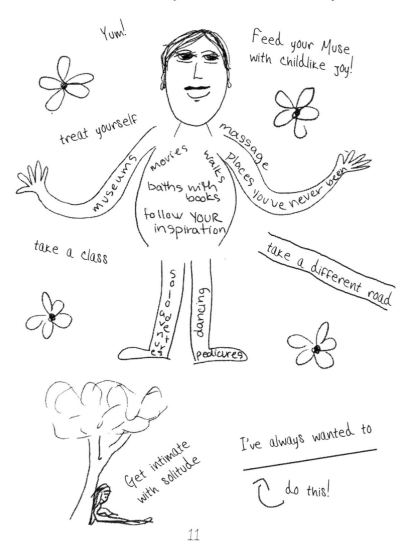

You might
be thinking...

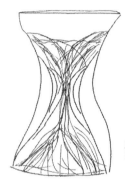

Yikes! Time is running out!
No time to be creative!
My phone is ringing now!
My kid needs me now!
Facebook is calling me now!

But actually,
a simple and
satisfying doodle
can be made
in five seconds.

 ← See?

So...

— shall we go?

I don't know if I can do this.

Don't worry.

We'll go together.

♡ ♡ ♡
Just turn the page.

THE PROMPTS

1.

Doodle something abstract, using shapes and only one color.

2.
Doodle one of your favorite things to do.

3.

When you were a kid, what did you want to be when you grew up? Doodle it in the simple way a child would.

4.
Doodle something you love about yourself.

5.
Doodle a quiet moment.

6.
Doodle a pilgrimage you'd like to take.

1.
Doodle something you're trying to make a decision about.

8.
Doodle having everything you need.

9.

Doodle one of your unique strengths.

10.
Doodle something soothing.

11. Doodle yourself doing things to fill your creative spirit.

12.
Doodle something you'd love to cross off your list.

13.

Use your non-dominant hand to doodle a love note that you secretly would like to send.

14.
Doodle an everyday miracle.

15.
Doodle something you're nurturing within yourself.

16. What is your favorite thing about winter? Doodle it.

17.
Doodle a hat you'd love to wear.

#

What's an agreement in your life — official or unspoken — that you'd like to change? Doodle it.

19.

Doodle something you can see right now that you appreciate.

20.
Doodle a song you want to compose and sing.

21.

Doodle something you currently love about your life.

22.
Doodle your favorite vegetable having a conversation.

23.
Doodle yourself living a dream.

24.

What are you healing in your life? Doodle it.

25.

Doodle something you'd be good at that you haven't ever done.

26.

Give yourself credit for five things. Doodle one or a combination of them.

27.

Doodle a scene from a dream you can remember.

28.

What's something you love that you don't think you should? Doodle it.

29.
Doodle a creative companion for yourself.

30.

What is a priority for you right now? Doodle it.

31.
Doodle a seed you'd like to plant.

32.
Doodle something that makes you feel calm.

33.

Using your non-dominant hand, doodle something you'd really, really love to get paid to do.

34.
Doodle an awesome memory.

35.

Doodle the voice that criticizes your creativity.

36.
Doodle something you'd like to continue.

37.

List three of your favorite distractions. Doodle one or a combination.

38.

What would you like to say good riddance/farewell to? Put it in a doodle.

39.
Doodle what sounds really good right now.

40.
Doodle something you least want to do that's hanging out there to be done.

41.

Doodle some of your craziest super powers.

42.
Doodle a wish list of things you want.

43.

Make a simple doodle that shows how flexible, rigid, or in-between you are.

44.
Doodle a dream home with no limits.

45.

Doodle what you'd like to get away with. Use your non-dominant hand.

46.
Doodle something embarrassing.

47.
Doodle a secret identity.

48.

Take a moment to imagine your body is talking to you. Doodle what it says.

49.

Doodle something you would do if you knew you couldn't fail.

50.
Doodle what inspires you.

51.

Where in your life do you feel alone? Doodle it.

52.

Doodle an edible forest with all your favorite foods.

53.

Imagine that while you were sleeping all of your problems were solved. Doodle what your world would look like when you wake up.

54.
Doodle inner peace.

55.

Use your non-dominant hand to doodle peace on earth.

56.
Doodle something you want to try but feel a little nervous about.

57.

Doodle a memory of feeling warm, loved, and complete, with nothing to worry about.

Doodle a holiday you love celebrating.

59.
Doodle something you enjoyed about your day.

60.
Doodle a question you've been contemplating.

61.
Doodle freedom.

62.
Doodle a nap.

63.

Doodle something from your everyday life that turns you on.

64.
Doodle yourself using your favorite technology.

65.
Doodle something you're proud of.

66.
Doodle yourself interacting with someone you admire.

67.

Make a list of three dream jobs with no limits. Doodle one or a combination.

68.
Doodle something you shy away from.

69.
Doodle one of your earliest memories.

70.

What are you convinced is really wrong with you? Doodle it with your non-dominant hand.

71.
Doodle yourself doing something with your friends.

72.
What do you adore?
Doodle it.

73.
Doodle something you're grateful for.

74.
Doodle rest.

75.
Doodle an auspicious sign you've seen.

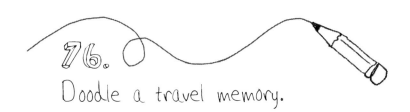

76.
Doodle a travel memory.

77.
Doodle a frame around an already existing doodle.

78.
Doodle an imagined success (something you haven't done yet).

79.
Doodle yourself giving a speech and show what it's about.

80.

Use your non-dominant hand to make a doodle of something you worry about.

81.
Doodle your most recent kiss.

82.
Doodle something you love about spring.

83.

Doodle yourself in your favorite piece of clothing.

84.

What is health to you?
Doodle it.

85.

Doodle something you like to do when you need a pick-me-up.

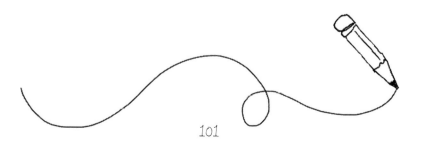

86.
Doodle one of your talents.

87.
Doodle your least favorite chore.

88.
Doodle your favorite chore.

89.
Doodle a situation where you typically act weird.

90.
Doodle something incorporating your favorite number.

91.
Doodle a happy surprise.

92.
What's on your mind?
Doodle it.

93.
Doodle something you're excited to try.

94.
Doodle good fortune.

95.

Doodle the most boring thing you can think of, and make it exciting.

96.
Doodle a bedtime ritual.

97.

Make a doodle to congratulate yourself for something.

Doodle yourself with someone who makes you feel starstruck.

99.
Doodle silence.

100.
What is something you can forgive yourself for?
Doodle it.

101.

Doodle your favorite body part. If it could talk, what would it say?

102.
Doodle yourself being of use.

103.

Pick your three favorite colors and let them inspire a free-form doodle.

104.
Doodle a recurring image that appears in your mind.

105.
Doodle something you've stolen.

106.

Doodle a teacher who had, or is having, a positive influence on you.

107.
Doodle a setting where you feel at home.

108.
Doodle a costume you'd like to dress up in.

109.

What emotion are you experiencing right now? Doodle a picture of where you feel it in your body.

110.

With your non-dominant hand, make a doodle to express gratitude for something.

III.
Doodle help.

112.

Doodle the cover of a book you'd like to write.

113.

Doodle something fun you have done for money.

114.

List three of your favorite childhood toys. Doodle one or a combination of them.

115.

Doodle yourself taking a time-out.

116.
Doodle something you wanted and now have.

117.

What's your favorite time of day? Doodle it.

118.

Doodle something really, really big interacting with something really, really small.

119.
Doodle an anniversary that you note each year.

120. What does willingness look like? Doodle it.

121.

Doodle something you've been keeping to yourself.

122.

Doodle yourself playing a musical instrument you've never played before.

123.
Doodle something that's a challenge for you.

124.

What are you doing well in life? Doodle yourself doing that.

125.
Doodle something you daydream about.

126.

Make a list of five things that are currently important to you. Doodle one or a combination of them.

127.
Doodle something you wonder about.

128.
Doodle your ideal support team.

129.
Doodle a comforting message to yourself.

130.

Using your non-dominant hand, doodle a quick self-portrait.

131.

Trace something and use its shape to spark a new doodle.

132.
Doodle a synchronicity you experienced that was especially magical.

133.

Doodle one of your strongest influences, such as a teacher, musician, author, poet, etc.

134.
Doodle magic.

135.

Doodle something with both hands, using shapes and colors.

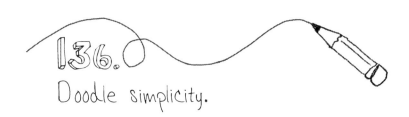

136.
Doodle simplicity.

137.
Doodle something that brings you joy.

138.
Doodle a wonderful gift you have received.

139.

What does relief look like?
Doodle it.

140. Doodle something you'd like to get better at doing.

141.

What did you like to draw as a child? Doodle it.

142.

Doodle something you'd like to do that seems daunting. Make this an "after" picture, as if the task is now completed.

143.

Do you consider yourself introverted, extroverted, or a combination? Show it in a very simple doodle. Try using stick figures.

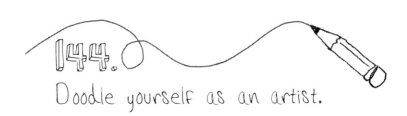

144.
Doodle yourself as an artist.

145.
Doodle something that's comforting to think about.

146.
Doodle yourself unwinding.

147.

If you were a plant, where would you like to be planted? Doodle the setting.

148.
Doodle an animal you have known and loved.

149.
Doodle something you can hear right now.

150.
Doodle generous self-appreciation.

151.

Go outside and make a quick doodle of something you see.

152.
Doodle what makes you feel free.

153.

Fill in the blank and doodle it: "Maybe I should _____."

154.

Doodle something new you've done recently. Bonus if it was today!

155.

Imagine your discouraging thoughts are food for a monster. Doodle that monster eating them.

156.

Doodle something you do regularly that you feel good about doing.

157.
Doodle someone who has encouraged you.

158.
Doodle someone being kind to you.

159.

Using your non-dominant hand, doodle a funny story you like to tell.

160.
Doodle love.

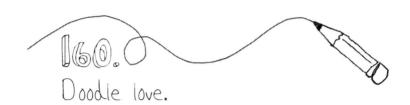

161.
Doodle being in a group.

162.
Doodle being alone.

163.

Doodle something in your present situation that you're resisting.

164. Invent a new sport that you'd be a champion at. Doodle it.

165.
Doodle something you'd like help with.

166.

What do you love about this moment? Doodle it!

167.

Pick a color and doodle the first thing that color reminds you of.

168.
Doodle something that got better.

169.

Doodle a simple image of you relaxing all tension.

170.

Where do you want to go on your next trip? Doodle it.

171.
Doodle something easy.

172.
Doodle a favorite concert memory.

173.

What can you count on?
Doodle it.

174.

Write down three things you're afraid of. Doodle one or a combination.

175.

Doodle an occupation you'd be surprised to find yourself doing.

176.

What do you remember about your earliest crush? Doodle the memory.

177.
Doodle something that is empty.

178.

Doodle someone who is a champion for you – someone who says "Yes!" to you.

179.
Doodle an object of comfort that soothes you.

180.
If you were a merchant, doodle what you would sell.

181.
Doodle yourself doing something outside.

182.
Doodle a recent fun memory.

183.
Doodle something you love to do but don't do very often.

184.
Doodle how your day started.

185.

What present would you like to receive right now? Show it in a doodle.

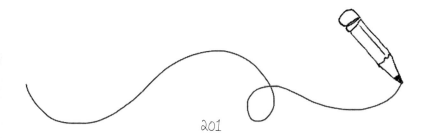

186.
Doodle something that makes you smile.

187.
Doodle a picture of a road leading into a magical land.

188. Doodle a house fairy to help you with all your chores.

189.
Doodle something you really like to touch.

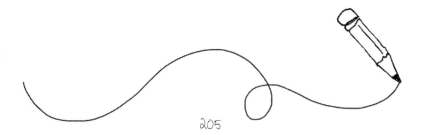

190.
Doodle a favorite spot in nature.

191.

Look around you and doodle something that catches your eye.

192.

What would you like to be free to do? List three things and doodle one or a combination.

193.
Doodle something that always makes you laugh.

194.

Doodle yourself with someone you'd love to have as a mentor.

195.
Doodle absent-mindedly.

196.
Doodle something you heard about that sounds fun.

197.

Doodle some ways life loves you right now.

198.
Doodle a departure.

199.
Doodle a place you'd like to return to.

200.
Doodle something that makes you blush.

201.
Doodle a monster you'd like to be friends with.

202.
Doodle a sound you find soothing.

203.

Doodle something you've been talking about doing.

204.

On a surface you don't typically doodle on, doodle a message you'd like to give the world.

205.
Doodle yourself doodling.

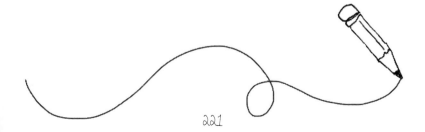

206.
Doodle something awkward.
Put in lots of detail.

207.

Make a gratidoodle, including as many things as you can think of.

208. Doodle a fun way to express anger.

209.
Doodle a party.

210.

What makes you happy?
Doodle that.

211.

Doodle something blue. If you don't have anything blue to draw with, use the colors you have to doodle something that's typically blue.

212.

Name three things you admire about yourself. Doodle one or a combination.

213.

Doodle a message to yourself from your future self.

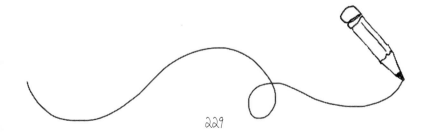

214.
Doodle yourself giving.

215.
Doodle yourself receiving.

216.
Doodle an activity that relaxes your mind.

217.
Doodle how you imagine someone else sees you.

218.

What message would you like to hear from the Universe? Doodle it.

219.
Doodle something that helps you fall asleep.

220.
Doodle an indulgence.

221.

Use your non-dominant hand to write the first word that comes to mind then make a doodle out of it.

222.
Doodle some of your favorite flowers.

223.

Doodle something you liked to pretend when you were a child.

224.
Doodle an intention for the day.

225.

Doodle something you can't comprehend.

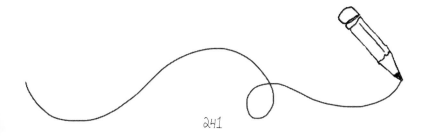

226.

Fill in the blank and doodle the following: "If nothing was holding me back, I would _____."

227.
Doodle nighttime.

228.
Doodle something in your life you'd be happy to outsource.

229.

Doodle a letter you've been meaning to write.

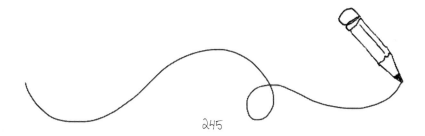

230.

Doodle an expression of thanks to someone who has helped you.

Doodle something effortless.

232.
Doodle a friend.

233.

If you went traveling, what gift would you like to bestow upon your hosts? Doodle it.

234.

Doodle a favorite food from childhood.

235.
Doodle a hug.

236.
Doodle something you are glad you did.

237.
Spend $10,000 in a doodle.

238.

Doodle something you tend to judge negatively about others.

239.

Doodle something you tend to judge negatively about yourself.

240.
Doodle the most peaceful thing you can think of.

241.

Turn on any song from the beginning and doodle along to it.

242.

Doodle your answer to this question: What do you do?

243.
Doodle something you have traded.

244. Doodle a blessing to yourself.

245.

Imagine you made a YouTube video that went viral. What is it about? Doodle a scene from it.

246.
Doodle something you've been meaning to get to.

247.
Doodle being totally off duty.

248.

Take five deep breaths. Now doodle the first thing that comes to mind.

249.

Doodle something that was easy to manifest.

250.
Doodle a summertime memory.

251.
Doodle mixed feelings.

252.
Doodle something you've accomplished.

253.
Doodle your version of a personal sanctuary.

254.

Doodle a small step to take in a direction you've been wanting to move.

255.

Imagine you are totally free of all obligations. Doodle the wildest thing you can think of to do.

256.
Doodle something you feel jealous about.

257.

Pretend you're observing yourself from the outside. Doodle what you see that you admire.

258.

Doodle something you're self-conscious about.

259.
Doodle a picture of yourself holding a sign that says "Everything is all right."

260.
What have you been ignoring?
Doodle it.

261.

Doodle something you worried about that worked out better than you expected.

262.

Doodle one of the great loves of your life.

263.

Use your non-dominant hand to doodle something you really want to say.

264.
Doodle a small task.

265.
Doodle something mysterious.

266.

Doodle a habit you have mixed feelings about.

267.
Doodle something you love about the world.

268. Think of someone you'd like to collaborate with. Doodle yourselves creating together.

269.

Doodle something in your life that was clearly meant to be.

270.
Doodle your first dance.

271.

Doodle yourself doing something completely out of character.

272.
Doodle someone who's easy to love.

273.
Doodle something that makes you feel better.

274.

Doodle as if you are leaving graffiti on a bathroom wall with a permanent marker.

275.

Doodle something worth celebrating.

276.
Doodle a picture of what you spend most of your money on.

277.

Make a doodle incorporating the sun.

278.

Doodle something that gives you butterflies in your stomach.

279.
Doodle a thank you note to an inanimate object.

280.

Doodle something that makes you stand out from others.

281.

Doodle a magic object you can carry with you.

282.

Doodle something you used to love doing that doesn't turn you on anymore.

283.

What's the nicest thing you can do for yourself right now? Show it in a doodle.

284.
With your non-dominant hand, doodle a solution to one of the world's major problems.

285.

Doodle an emoji of how you feel in this moment.

286.
Doodle something that comes naturally to you.

287.
Doodle a place where everybody has a good time.

288. What does it look like inside your mind right now? Doodle it.

289.
Doodle your favorite song.

290.
Doodle self-love.

291.
Doodle yourself as the boss of something.

292.
Doodle your to-do list using silly pictures.

293.

If you were a rock star on tour, what would insist on having in your dressing room at every venue? Doodle it.

294.
Doodle something you're obsessed with.

295.
Doodle your favorite food winning an award.

296.
Doodle a shape or object or word repeatedly. Fill the page with it.

297.

Doodle something quirky about yourself that most people don't know.

298.
Doodle how you like to bathe.

299.
Doodle what you would do with a magic wand.

300.
Doodle something you are in awe of.

301.

Use your non-dominant hand to doodle something that is definitely good for your mind, body, and spirit.

302.
Doodle an animal.
Bonus: make up a new one.

303.

Doodle a charity or service organization that you'd like to support.

304.
Doodle an award for yourself.

305.
Doodle an award for someone else.

306.

What do you know well enough to teach? Doodle that.

307.

Doodle what it was like to finally do something you'd been meaning to do for awhile.

308.
Doodle a habit you've had since childhood.

309.
Doodle yourself interacting with a fictional character.

310.

Call to mind something you've done that was really cool and fun but you don't think about it often. Doodle it.

311.
Doodle a great idea.

312.
Doodle yourself on an awesome road trip.

313.

What's something that's challenging for you, but you're doing it and getting better at it anyway?

314.

What does autumn make you think of? Doodle it.

315.

Doodle a futuristic household item.

316.
Doodle something you like to meditate on.

317.

What are you ready for more of? Doodle it.

318.

What are you ready to take a break from? Doodle it.

319.

Close your eyes and make a mark on a page, using a few twists and turns. Open your eyes and finish your doodle.

320.
Doodle a friendly version of something that's typically scary.

321.

Doodle how you imagine yourself at your best.

322.

Think of an object you use every day. Doodle a picture of it talking.

323.

Doodle something you like to collect.

324.
Doodle a luxuriously relaxing scene.

325.

What does empathy look like to you? Doodle that.

326.

Doodle evidence that you are on the right path.

327.

Doodle where you'd like to travel in a time machine.

328.
Doodle something that you're good at attracting.

329.

Doodle yourself prepared to receive what you've been wanting.

330.
Imagine you and your dream dinner date are forming a new business together. Doodle it.

331.

Doodle something you've done today that you feel good about, no matter how big or how small.

332.
Doodle someone you have a crush on.

333.
Doodle some thoughts that tell you it's not ok to rest.

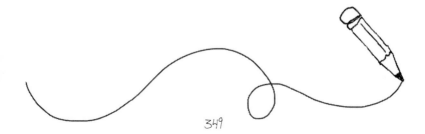

334.

Doodle something that feels good.

335.

List three or more things that are already working in your favor. Doodle one or a combination.

336.

Using your non-dominant hand, doodle something you'd like to shout really loudly.

337.
Doodle a memory from a favorite book.

338.
Doodle something fun.

339.
Doodle a brilliant invention that solves a common problem.

340.
Doodle your own version of a favorite piece of art.

341.

Make a doodle for someone else and give it to them.

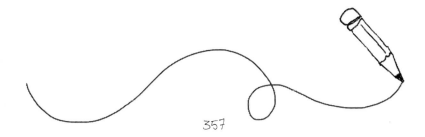

342.
Doodle something that you've mastered.

343.

Doodle a circle, a triangle, and a rectangle. Use your imagination to connect them.

344.
Doodle something nice about your day.

345.
Doodle your favorite weather.

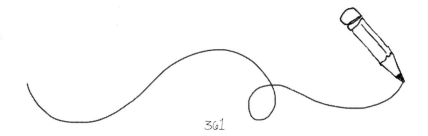

346.
Doodle something you do every day.

347.
Doodle a place you regularly go in your neighborhood.

348.

What's something on your mind that you tend to keep to yourself? Reveal it in a doodle.

349.

What does your world look like if you have no limitations? Doodle it.

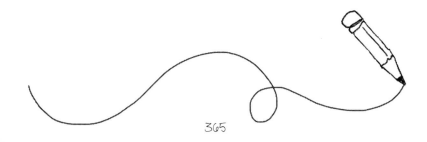

350.
Doodle something to hang on the refrigerator.

351.

Thank yourself for five things. Doodle one or a combination of them.

352.

Doodle yourself doing two of your favorite activities that you wouldn't normally do together.

353.

What's a big pressure in your life? Doodle yourself easing off of it.

354.

Doodle something in your future going extraordinarily well.

355.
Doodle a picture of yourself feeling appreciation.

356.
Doodle a quiet mind.

357.

What helps you feel connected to others? Doodle it.

358.

Doodle an outlandish solution to a conflict in your life.

359.

Doodle a conversation you've imagined having with someone that hasn't happened yet.

360. Pretend you've been made boss of the world. Doodle what you would do first.

361.
Doodle what you imagine keeps you from your dreams.

362.

Doodle something you didn't know you could do, but you did it.

363.
Doodle a way you like to exercise.

364.
Celebrate something about yourself in a doodle.

365.
Doodle your feelings about doodling.

366. (And one for leap year) Imagine you are a hero returning from an adventure. Doodle the gifts you bring home.

Keep doodling!

"Follow your bliss...
and don't be afraid
to follow it."
—Joseph Campbell

GRATITUDE

My love for doodling was sparked by a question in the book *The Artist's Way*. Big thanks to author Julia Cameron for asking the right questions (and for teaching me what makes a good prompt). The spark turned to fire with that first 30 Day Doodle Challenge invitation from melissaAnne Colors. My gratitude is bigger than I can put into words.

I'm eternally grateful for every meal, juice, treat, conversation, and place to rest my head. Loving thanks to Giraffe & Lion, Maureen Ananda, Brian, DR, JB, Jesse, Jenny, Meowmee, Sadie, and Michael Ann. Your love, confidence, and encouragement is immeasurable. Look at what we made!

To MF: You've been with me all along. Thank you for giving me a worthy subject for expression.

To Shelley Arenas of Intentional Publishing for providing a loving space for this book to be born into. Thanks for getting me! Thank you Julie-Anne Graham for putting the pieces together in such an uplifting way.

To B.J. Fogg and your TED Talk for brilliantly teaching me how to get the prompts written.

To Joe Cross ("Joe the Juicer") for encouraging me to gather my team and to begin Doodling with Strangers.

To all of the Stranger Doodlers and Doodle Booth friends: Your generous participation inspires me and validates the doodle vision every day, and I am so grateful.

And to Mom, Dad & Squirtle. Love love love.

Doodle Outreach

Doodling connects people in unexpected ways. Your experience with the prompts in this book may inspire you to introduce daily doodling at work or at the dinner table. You may become a Doodle Outreach Ambassador and share the gift of simple expression with everyone you meet.

Here I am Doodling with Strangers (I recommend it!): www.youtube.com/doodlingwithstrangersfun

Join me and fellow doodlers from all over the world on Facebook at www.facebook.com/groups/doodleoutreach

Share your doodles and stories by writing to

Doodle Outreach
c/o Intentional Publishing
P.O. Box 55872
Seattle, WA 98155

or by emailing carin@doodleoutreach.com

For further creativity encouragement, visit www.doodleoutreach.com

Made in the USA
Charleston, SC
06 December 2015